STUPENDOUS
SCIENCE

Rob Beattie

illustrated by Sam Peet

First published in the United States by QEB Publishing, Inc.

Part of The Quarto Group
6 Orchard,
Lake Forest, CA 92630

A CIP record for this book is available from the Library of Congress.

ISBN: 978 1 68297 257 1

10 9 8 7 6 5 4 3 2

Manufactured in Guangdong, China TT112017

Editor: Nancy Dickmann
Project Editor: Carly Madden
Editorial Director: Laura Knowles
Art Director: Susi Martin
Publisher: Maxime Boucknooghe
Production: Nikki Ingram
Consultant: Pete Robinson

CONTENTS ...

INTRODUCTION

Welcome to Stupendous Science! This book will show you that the everyday objects lying around the house—things that you don't think twice about—are actually completely amazing.

You'll unlock the secrets inside stuff like water, air, salt, sugar, and dozens of other easy-to-get-hold-of items. In the right hands (that means your hands!) these items can do astounding things.

Experimenting!

In this book you'll find a wide range of experiments that give you a chance to explore chemistry, physics, biology, and engineering. Within those categories there are some short experiments as well as some longer ones. Some are straightforward and some are more challenging. There are also lots that are just plain good fun—they'll make you laugh as well as think!

Below each page number, you will find one of four symbols. This lets you know in which science category the experiment belongs.

chemistry   physics   biology   engineering

Take it Further

These boxes will show you how to take the experiment a step further and develop your scientific skills.

What's the Science?

Look out for the boxes that accompany each experiment. They'll explain the fascinating science behind each project and help you to understand exactly what's going on. The "In the real world" boxes look at the ways that the experiment can be applied in real life.

Safety First

We've used a simple color-coding system to label each experiment, showing whether or not you need adult supervision. The colors are on the page numbers. Here's how it works:

Green—no adults required! You're on your own, so knock yourself out (just don't literally knock yourself out). But check with an adult first before you start experimenting!

Yellow—some of the steps require an adult to supervise or actually do them. They usually involve knives or fire or a substance that needs handling with care.

Red—you must have an adult on hand for this experiment. Do not try and do this on your own because some or all of the steps require help or supervision.

Make sure to follow any health and safety advice—especially wearing rubber gloves or goggles where it says to! Never buy any equipment or ingredients online without an adult's permission.

To understand science is to understand how the world works. This book will help you to take the first steps on an exciting journey of discovery that could lead you...well, anywhere!

Ready to get started?

FANTASTIC FIZZY FOUNTAIN

This experiment uses two familiar ingredients which, when mixed together, produce a fizzy fountain that rockets into the air. Do this outside—it's messy!

You Will Need
- large bottle of cola
- packet of Mentos sweets
- flat surface

What's the Science?
Although they look smooth, Mentos are covered in a gazillion tiny little bumps. These attract the bubbles (made of carbon dioxide) in the cola, which in turn attract other bubbles. This chain reaction quickly gets out of control, causing the bottle to erupt.

1 Take the bottle and the Mentos outside and place the bottle on a firm, flat surface.

2 Take a mint out of the packet, ready for Step 3. Unscrew the top of the bottle.

3 Drop the mint into the open bottle and stand back.

4 THERE SHE BLOWS!

Take it Further If you like this volcanic experiment, you could try it out using different carbonated drinks, or different kinds of mints. Which combination sets off the biggest reaction? Which one is a feeble flop? Remember to make a note of your results and conclusion!

HOMEMADE HOVERCRAFT

Do you like the idea of having a toy that glides silently across the kitchen counter?

You Will Need
- old CD or DVD
- round balloon
- superglue
- pull-up top from a water bottle

1 Make sure the pull-up top is closed. Unscrew it from the bottle and remove its small plastic cap.

2 Get an adult to "paint" some superglue around the bottom of the bottle top.

3 Push the bottle top onto the CD/DVD, making sure it covers the hole and that there are no gaps for air to get in. Wait five minutes to make sure the glue has dried.

4 Blow up the balloon and place it over the top of the bottle top.

5 Pull the bottle top up and take your hand away.

What's the Science?

Friction is the word scientists use to describe the resistance you get when one surface moves across another. Try to slide a CD across a surface, and friction will slow it down. Introducing a flow of air reduces this friction, which allows the CD to glide along much more smoothly.

6 Off goes the hovercraft!

PEEPING PERISCOPE ☉ ☉

**Want to see over fences or around corners?
You, my friend, need a periscope.**

You will need
- two empty one-quart milk or juice cartons
- two small, square mirrors or mirror tiles, about the same width as the carton
- utility knife
- ruler
- pen or pencil
- masking tape

1 Ask an adult to cut very carefully around the top of each carton to remove the end that you pour from. (An adult should do all the cutting in this activity.) Wash and dry both cartons.

2 Take one of the cartons and measure 1/4 inch up from the closed end and cut a square hole in one side. Be sure to leave 1/4 inch on the left and right edges of the hole.

3 Lay the carton on its side with the hole facing to the right, then measure 1/4 inch up from the bottom of the left edge and make a mark with your pen.

In the Real World
Although now there are more modern alternatives, periscopes are still used by many submarines to see what's around them without having to actually come up to the surface.

4 Draw a line from the mark you just made down to the opposite bottom corner—it should make a right angle triangle.

5 Cut along this line with the knife. The cut needs to be just long enough and wide enough to accommodate one of the mirrors.

6 Slide the mirror into the slot so the reflective side is facing the hole you cut in Step 2. Watch out for sharp edges!

7 Tape the mirror loosely into place.

9 Take the two cartons and fit one inside the other so that the hole in the bottom one is facing you and the hole in the top one is facing away from you.

10 Hold the cartons in position while you look through the hole to make sure everything works. Adjust the mirrors if you need to.

8 Look through the hole and make sure you can see the ceiling through the mirror. If you can't, adjust the mirror. Repeat Steps 2–8 with the other carton and mirror.

11 Tape the mirror firmly in place, tape the two cartons together, and you have your periscope!

What's the Science?

It's all to do with the way light reflects back from a mirror. It always reflects at the same angle as it "hits" the mirror. If your mirrors are angled at 45 degrees, light will hit the top mirror, bounce off at a right angle and travel straight down the periscope to hit the second mirror, where it bounces off at another right angle toward your eye.

TWISTED TASTE BUDS

So you think you can tell the difference between an apple and a pear? They look different—obviously!—and they taste different, too. At least, that's what you might think. This experiment will show you how wrong you are!

You Will Need
- very ripe apple
- pear
- vegetable peeler
- sharp knife

1 Peel the apple and the pear carefully.

2 Ask an adult to help you cut them into pieces.

3 Take a bite of the pear. Once that's done, take a bite of apple. It's easy to tell the difference, isn't it?

4 Now pinch your nose tight and repeat Step 3.

What's the Science?
You need both the taste buds on your tongue and the smell sensors inside your nose to identify what something tastes like. If you can't smell anything, then two foods with the same texture will taste pretty much the same.

5 The pear and apple should now taste the same.

WOW!

THE GETAWAY GRAPE

Would you believe it if someone told you that grapes are magnetic? Surely it sounds too bizarre to be true. After all, you can't stick a grape to your fridge...

1 Carefully slide one of the grapes onto each end of the straw.

2 Hold out your finger and place the middle of the straw on the end of it, so that the straw balances.

You Will Need
- two grapes
- drinking straw
- neodymium magnet (you can buy these strong magnets— sometimes called "rare-earth magnets"— online, or an adult may be able to help you find some already being used in your house)

THAT'S AMAZING!

3 With your other hand, move the magnet near a grape but don't touch it—the grape will move away from the magnet.

What's the Science?

Grapes are mainly made of water, which is diamagnetic. This means it will be repelled by both poles of a magnet. Diamagnetism is very weak, which is why you need a strong magnet for the experiment to work.

Take it Further
Try other fruits that contain different amounts of water (such as a piece of apple or a prune). Compare how they react to the magnet.

SERIOUSLY SLIMY

Close your eyes and imagine the ooziest, most gooey, most disgusting gunk you can think of. Now let's make some!

You Will Need
- white glue
- borax substitute (it's actually called that)
- food coloring (optional)
- rubber gloves
- water
- two bowls
- something to stir with
- measuring cup

1 In the first bowl, mix half a cup of water and half a cup of glue.

2 If you want to make colored slime, add a few drops of food coloring.

3 Put on the rubber gloves. In the second bowl, mix one cup of water with one teaspoon of borax substitute until it dissolves.

In the Real World

Want to discover the king of slime? Meet the hagfish, a strange eel-like creature that lives in the sea and feeds on the insides of dead fish. When attacked, hagfish can produce enough defensive slime to choke a shark. Hagfish slime is made of incredibly tiny but strong threads. Scientists are trying to figure out whether it can be used to make useful stuff—like sturdy outdoor clothing, for example. It would certainly make a great bungee-jumping rope!

4 Now, take the first bowl and pour the contents into the second bowl, stirring all the time.

5 Goo-tastic slime will start to form as soon as you mix the contents of the two bowls. Keep stirring!

6 Finish off the mixing with your gloved hands to make perfect, long-lasting slime.

Health and Safety

Although not dangerous, borax substitute should be handled with care. That's why we're using rubber gloves—and you should wash thoroughly after this experiment. You'd have to accidentally eat lots of borax substitute for it to do you any lasting harm and since it tastes horrible and soapy, no one would! It can irritate the skin a bit, so watch out for that.

What's the Science?

Craft glue is also called PVA glue. PVA stands for polyvinyl acetate, which is a liquid polymer. This is a chemical compound with rubbery, elastic qualities because of the way its molecules are chained together. The borax substitute links these chains to produce even more elasticity. The result is something you can mold with your hands or leave on a flat surface, where it will ooze into a puddle!

WORKING WALKIE-TALKIE

This simple walkie-talkie may seem low-tech, but it's how your parents talked to each other before cell phones! (OK... maybe not!)

1 Use the skewer to poke a small hole in the bottom of each cup. The hole should be in the middle.

2 Poke one end of the string through the hole and into the cup. Tie a knot on the inside so the string won't get pulled out.

3 Repeat Step 2 for the other cup.

4 Pull the string tight between the two cups.

You Will Need
- two paper cups
- some string
- skewer (or something else to poke a hole in the cups)

5 As you speak into one cup, get your friend to hold their cup up to their ear.

What's the Science?

When you speak, your voice makes the bottom of the cup vibrate with sound waves. The waves travel down the tight string and make the bottom of the second cup vibrate. The sound of your voice comes out of the other end for your friend to hear.

TWIRLY BIRDS

Helicopters use rotor blades to take off and hover. You can make your own simple helicopter-style spinner in just a few moments.

You Will Need
- **rectangular piece of paper (white or colored)**
- **paper clip**
- **pair of scissors**

1 Starting about one-third of the way along the short end of the paper, make the first cut like this. You should stop cutting before you reach the edge of the paper.

2 Turn the paper around and make a second cut, just like the first one.

3 Pick up the two ends, one in each hand.

4 Put the two ends together.

5 Secure the ends with the paper clip.

6 Toss your Twirly Bird into the air and watch it spin slowly to the ground.

What's the Science?

As it spins, the Twirly Bird acts like a helicopter. It generates lift—a force that pushes upward and slows its descent.

Take it Further Experiment with different sizes and weights of paper and paper clip to make more Twirly Birds. Watch how the different materials and sizes affect how long your "bird" stays in the air.

COLORING CARNATIONS

See that white flower? Boring, huh? So let's turn it into something a bit more interesting...

You Will Need
- white flower—something like a carnation is good
- two tall glasses of the same size
- jug of water
- food coloring in bright colors such as red, yellow, or blue
- sharp knife (if you're not allowed to use one on your own, get an adult to help with this experiment)

1 Cut the stem of the flower at an angle. You want the stem to be slightly taller than the glass.

2 Fill one glass with water and put the flower into it.

3 Fill the other glass with water and then add a few drops of food coloring. Stir it to mix it in.

4 Take the flower out of the first glass. Carefully cut the stem straight down the middle, starting at the bottom and going up to about 2 inches from the flower head.

5 Place the two glasses next to each other, then "open" the stem carefully and place one half in one glass and the other in the second glass.

6 After a couple of days, half of the flower will change color!

What's the Science?

When tiny molecules of water move through a plant (this is called transpiration), they pull up other water molecules through the stem to take their place. It is called cohesion, because water molecules like to "stick" to each other. How can the water travel up the stem against gravity? Because water not only sticks to itself, but also to other things—like the stem of the flower. Try dipping a paper towel in water and watch it climb up the fibers!

P.S. Were you wondering why you need to cut the stem at an angle in Step 1? It's because that gives the stem more surface area with which to absorb water from the glass.

THE CHRONO-COMPASS

Let's navigate the old-fashioned way, using nothing more than sunlight and a simple watch.

You Will Need
- an analog watch (one with hands)
- sunlight

1 Hold the watch flat in your hand and turn it until the hour hand is pointing at the sun.

Remember: never look directly at the sun!

2 If it's before noon, look at the hour hand and let your eyes travel clockwise around the watch's face until you reach 12:00. Now imagine a line running through the midpoint between the two locations. If it's after noon, let your eyes travel counterclockwise instead.

3 The imaginary line running through the middle point between the hour hand and 12:00 points south. The imaginary line running in the opposite direction points to the north.

4 Note: if you are in the southern hemisphere, then line up the 12:00 mark with the sun and measure to the hour hand, instead.

What's the Science?

The sun is predictable. It always rises in the east and sets in the west, so it's possible to use its path to find north, south, east, and west.

ICE CUBES AWAY!

Pick up an ice cube with only a matchstick? That's impossible, isn't it?

You Will Need
- bowl of water
- matchstick*
- ice cube
- table salt

WOW!

1 Place the ice cube carefully into the bowl of water.

2 Gently place the match lengthwise on top of it and try to use it to lift the ice cube.

3 It doesn't work, does it? Now put the matchstick back and this time sprinkle a little salt along the line where it touches the ice cube.

4 Wait about 30 seconds and try again. You'll be able to lift the ice cube out of the water!

In the Real World

This is more than just a cool trick. It shows why we sprinkle salt on icy roads—it melts the ice.

*instead of using a matchstick, you can also try this experiment using a piece of string.

What's the Science?

At first, the ice cube and water are in "equilibrium," meaning that the rate of freezing and melting is the same. Adding the salt lowers the rate at which the water freezes, so the ice melts faster. This releases lots of energy in the form of heat, so everything gets colder, including the ice cube. Where there's no salt (under the match) the ice cube re-freezes, freezing the match in place.

THE SOLAR OVEN

If you want to try cooking your food using only the power of the sun, you've come to the right place.

You will need
- empty pizza box, the bigger the better
- pencil or pen
- utility knife
- aluminum foil
- white glue
- plastic wrap
- black tape
- some black paper
- plastic straw

1 Draw a square on the top of the pizza box that's about 1 inch from each edge.

2 Have an adult help you cut along three sides of the square you just drew—all except the line nearest the hinge of the pizza box.

3 Open the flap you've just created.

In the Real World

Campers and hikers can buy solar ovens that will cook food in minutes. They have built-in vacuum tubes which are almost perfect insulators, so none of the captured heat can escape.

4 Cover the inside of the flap with foil, folding it around the edges and securing it in place with the glue.

5 Use the plastic wrap to cover the opening beneath the flap, taping it in place. Make sure there are no holes in the plastic wrap.

6 Open the pizza box completely and then line the inside (the bottom, sides, and the lid) with foil. Glue it into place (obviously, don't put foil over the plastic wrap).

7 Line the bottom of the inside of the pizza box with black paper and glue it into place.

8 Place your "oven" in bright sunlight. Use the straw to prop the flap open so that the foil on the underside of the flap reflects sunlight into the oven.

9 Pre-heat for about 30 minutes, then put your food inside. How about a chocolate chip cookie and marshmallow sandwich? Warning: do not use your oven for meat or other foods that can make you sick if they aren't fully cooked.

DELICIOUS!

What's the Science?

Earth gets more energy from the sun in one hour than the entire planet uses in a year. The heat from the sun hits the foil on the flap. It is reflected into the box, where it heats the air that's trapped inside. Why the black paper? Because black is great at absorbing heat and converting light into heat. The foil inside the oven also helps prevent the heat from escaping. An oven like this can reach over 200 degrees Fahrenheit on a clear sunny day, so be careful!

THE CHARISMATIC COMB

Combs are very useful for keeping your hair neat, but are they attractive as well? Try this, and you'll see that water likes the look of your comb so much that it actually tries to move toward it!

You Will Need
- plastic comb
- cold water faucet
- some hair

1 Run the comb through your hair ten times.

x 10

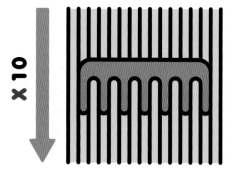

2 Run the cold water for ten seconds, then reduce the flow so that there's just enough pressure for a very gentle stream.

3 Hold the comb near the water.

4 Watch to see what happens. The water should bend toward the comb because it is attracted to it by the static charge.

What's the Science?

Running the comb through your hair creates static electricity: electrons which are negatively charged. Water molecules are neutral. When you move the comb near the water, it pushes away the negatively charged electrons and then attracts the remaining positive ones, so the water bends toward the comb.

BIG EYES, SMALL EYES

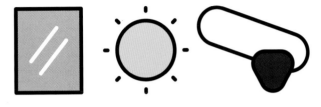

Your eyes always stay the same size, right? Wrong.

You Will Need
- a sunny day
- eyepatch
- mirror

4 The pupil is the dark circle in the middle of your eye. The pupil that was under the eyepatch will be much bigger than the other one.

1 Put the eyepatch over one eye. (Give yourself extra points for a hearty pirate "Arrrhh!")

ARRHHH!

2 Sit outside on a sunny day for five minutes. (DO NOT look straight at the sun.)

3 Go inside and stand in front of the mirror, then take off the eyepatch and examine both of your eyes.

What's the Science?

The only reason you can see anything is because objects reflect light. Your pupil's job is to let in as much light as you need in order to see stuff. So, in sunlight, it gets smaller because you don't need as much light. But in darkness (like under that eyepatch) it gets bigger because it's trying to let in as much light as possible.

SMARTPHONE PROJECTOR

If you want to create your own home movie theater with a cell phone and a few other bits and pieces, then read on...

You Will Need
- shoebox (preferably one that has dark insides)
- magnifying glass (that you can unscrew from its handle)
- two good-sized binder clips
- craft knife (and an adult to use it)
- electrical tape
- pencil
- smartphone
- empty white wall or a white sheet

1 With the lid removed, stand the shoebox on one end.

2 Unscrew the handle and place the magnifying glass on the end of the shoebox, then draw around it with the pencil.

3 Ask an adult to cut out a magnifying glass-sized hole in the end of the box.

4 Tape the magnifying glass over the hole, inside and out, making sure there are no gaps.

5 Lay the shoebox flat and try to stand your smartphone up inside it (this may work if it has a hard case).

6 If the phone needs some help, take the two binder clips and position them as shown.

7 Stand the phone up on the clips. You want the screen to face directly at the magnifying glass, so it may need some adjusting.

8 If you try to watch something with your projector now, it'll come out upside down. Seriously. So find the setting that lets you rotate the phone's screen and lock it there—otherwise, the screen will keep trying to right itself.

9 Turn the phone's brightness up as far as it'll go, find a video and start playing it. As you do, pick up the shoebox and point it at the wall or sheet.

10 Starting from the opposite end of the room, walk toward the wall until the picture comes into focus.

11 Fine-tune the sharpness of the video by moving the phone forward or backward inside the box.

What's the Science?

When light passes through a lens (like a magnifying glass) it gets flipped so that images appear upside down. That's why you have to make sure your phone is upside down for the video to appear the right way up. Believe it or not, your eyes work the same way. Everything you see is actually upside down —it's just that your brain corrects the orientation automatically for you.

12 Put the lid back on the box, place it on a table, and grab the popcorn!

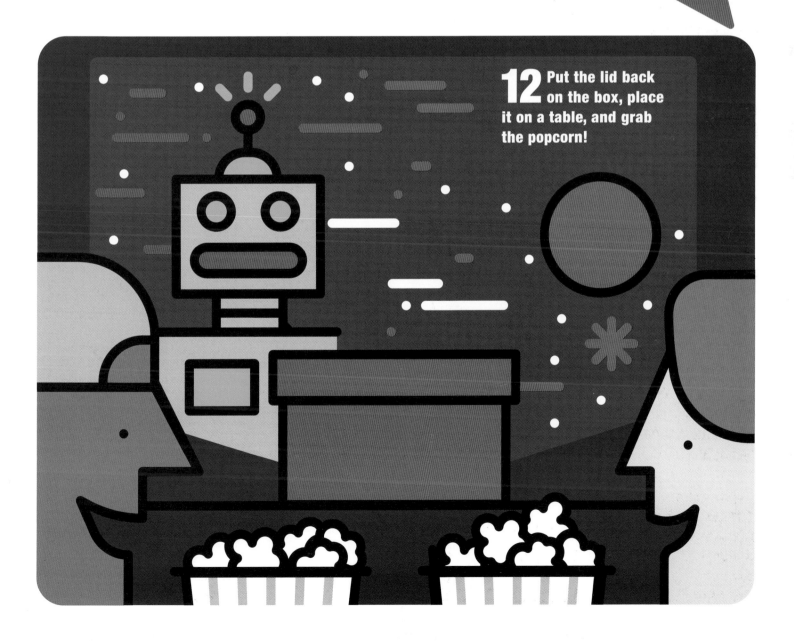

BENDY BONES

If you've ever wished you were strong enough to bend a bone in half, then wish no more.

1 Rinse the bone in water to get rid of any remaining meat.

2 Try bending the bone. Can't do it, huh?

You Will Need
- bowl
- vinegar
- chicken leg bone (from raw chicken)

3 Put it into the bowl and cover with the vinegar, then wash your hands. Leave it to soak for three days.

4 On the fourth day, take the bone out, rinse it, and try again. Success!

WOW!

What's the Science?

Your bones contain calcium carbonate, a key substance that makes them stronger. Vinegar, on the other hand, is an acid. It's strong enough to dissolve any calcium carbonate in the bone, but not strong enough to actually damage the bone. That's why you can bend it.

THAT SUCKS! AND BLOWS!

Here's how to suck an egg straight into a bottle without touching it!

You Will Need
- hard-boiled egg
- empty bottle (the opening needs to be just a bit smaller than the egg, so it can't fall through)
- scrap of paper
- lighter or matches

1 Peel the shell from the egg.

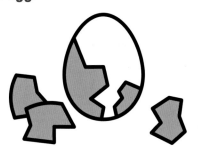

2 You'll need an adult to help you with the rest of the experiment. Have them light the scrap of paper and drop it into the bottle.

3 Rest the egg on top of the bottle as the paper burns.

4 The egg will be pulled into the bottle!

What's the Science?

Air inside the bottle expands when you add the burning paper. When the flame goes out, the air contracts. The pressure inside is now less than the pressure outside. It seems like the egg is sucked in, but it is pushed in by the higher pressure outside the bottle. When you blow into the bottle, you reverse the process, and the increased pressure inside pushes the egg back out.

Take it Further Carefully remove any pieces of burned paper, tip the bottle up to your lips, and blow into it for two seconds. Remove your mouth and the egg will slide back out of the bottle.

THE CONCEALED COIN

Here's how to tell which hand is hiding the coin—every time.

1 Pass the coin to your friend.

You Will Need
- coin
- helpful friend

2 Turn your back and close your eyes.

3 Ask them to close both hands into fists. Then they need to hold the hand with the coin in it above their head for one minute while you read their mind.

4 Tell them to hold both hands out in front of them. Now turn around and pick the hand that hides the coin.

What's the Science?
When your friend holds their hand above their head, the blood will drain slightly from that hand, leaving it paler than the other one. All you have to do is pick that hand and you'll find the coin every time!

In the Real World
Step 3 is tricky, because you need to distract your friend so they don't start to wonder why they have to hold their hand over their head for a minute. Try telling them how their mind is the hardest you've ever tried to read; anything to distract them. Magicians call this technique "misdirection."

THE THUNDEROUS TUBE

If you enjoy making a thunderous racket (and who doesn't?), then you're going to love this simple experiment.

You Will Need

- cardboard drum about 10 inches high and 6 inches across, ideally with a cardboard bottom (try a hobby store, search online, or ask your parents if they have an old gift box that had a bottle of wine in it)
- a spring about 18 inches long (sometimes called a coil spring or steel extension spring)
- a Phillips-style screwdriver

1 Carefully poke a hole in the bottom of the drum with the screwdriver. It should be slightly smaller than the diameter of the spring.

2 Poke one end of the spring into the hole and then turn it like you would turn a screw, so that about five turns are sticking through inside the drum.

3 Your thunder tube is ready! Hold the tube and shake it from side to side. You'll be amazed at the incredible noise it makes!

What's the Science?

As you shake the tube, the spring vibrates, which causes the bottom of the drum to vibrate as well. The tube amplifies the sound to produce that distinctive roll of thunder. Amazing!

ELEPHANT'S TOOTHPASTE

If elephants brushed their teeth, we're pretty sure that their tubes of toothpaste would look something like this!

You Will Need
- large empty bottle of soda or water
- 1/2 cup of 40 volume hydrogen peroxide (corrosive) —an adult can buy this from a beauty supply store
- about a tablespoon of dry yeast
- warm water
- some dishwashing liquid
- food coloring
- small cup
- tablespoon
- measuring jug
- plastic funnel (optional)
- safety goggles
- some outside space—it's going to get messy!

1 Put on your goggles and then ask an adult to measure out the hydrogen peroxide.

2 Ask them to pour the hydrogen peroxide into the empty bottle.

3 Add about 10 drops of food coloring to the bottle.

4 Add about a tablespoon of dishwashing liquid to the bottle.

5 Swirl it around to mix everything together.

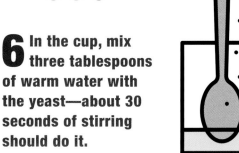

6 In the cup, mix three tablespoons of warm water with the yeast—about 30 seconds of stirring should do it.

7 Pour the yeast mixture into the bottle (use the funnel if you have one).

8 Stand back! The contents of the bottle will foam out of the top like toothpaste out of a tube, but ten times bigger. That's why it's called elephant's toothpaste!

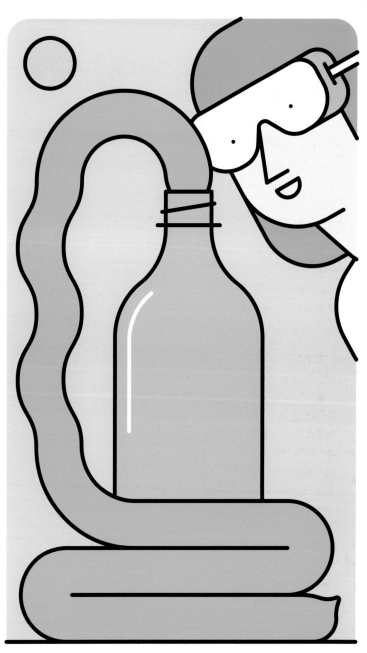

Take it Further When the "toothpaste" has stopped flowing, put your hand around the bottle and you'll find that it's warm. That's because your experiment has also produced heat—it's an exothermic reaction. This is the term scientists use to describe what happens when a chemical reaction releases energy in the form of heat.

What's the Science?

The yeast and water mixture acts as a catalyst—something that speeds up a chemical reaction in another substance, while remaining unchanged itself. When you add this to the bottle it makes the hydrogen peroxide break down into oxygen and water. The dishwashing liquid traps the oxygen in bubbles to create the foam. Just a small amount of hydrogen peroxide will create a lot of oxygen, so you get loads of bubbles—making your "toothpaste" almost explode out of the bottle.

BALANCING ACT

Balancing two forks on the edge of a glass with just a toothpick? You must be crazy. Crazy like a scientist, that is!

1 Take the two forks and interweave the prongs so they're nice and tight. You should be able to hold them both by one end when you're finished.

You Will Need
- glass tumbler
- two identical forks (they must be exactly the same)
- toothpick
- (optional) lighter or matches

2 Balance the forks on your finger to find the center of gravity.

3 Poke the toothpick through the prongs at the same position.

4 Balance the toothpick on the edge of the glass, moving it and the forks back and forth until you find the balance point.

What's the Science?

It's all about the center of gravity—sometimes called the center of mass. By finding this point, it's possible to balance something very heavy (like the forks) using something pretty flimsy (like the toothpick).

Take it Further With the forks balanced, ask an adult to light the end of the toothpick nearest to the center of the glass. Watch as it burns all the way through to the edge of the glass. Amazingly, thanks to physics, it will still balance the forks! WARNING! NEVER USE MATCHES, A LIGHTER, OR GO NEAR FIRE WITHOUT ADULT SUPERVISION.

PUNCH A POTATO

Anyone can punch a potato (if they really want to). But with a straw?

1 Hold the straw as though it was a dart or an arrow and try stabbing the potato as hard as you can.

2 Throw away your bent and broken straw! Now, if at first you don't succeed...

3 Cover one end of the straw with your thumb and try again.

4 This time you'll be able to pierce the skin without any problems.

What's the Science?

At first, the straw has no chance of piercing the potato because it's not strong enough. When you put your thumb over the top, you're trapping air inside the straw. This gets compressed sharply when you stab the potato, making the straw strong enough to pierce the skin.

RIGHT OR LEFT?

Do you favor your left side or your right side? These simple experiments will help you find out.

You Will Need
- notebook for your results
- pen or pencil
- ruler
- empty cardboard tube
- glass of water
- soft ball (like a Nerf ball)

1 Draw a couple of columns on the paper and label them "left" and "right." You'll use these to record the results of the experiments. Put a check mark in the relevant column as you answer each question.

What's the Science?

Some scientists believe that humans have a genetic bias toward right-handedness almost by accident. It turns out that the brain is cross-wired so that the left side controls the right side of our bodies, and vice versa. This left side also controls speech and language, without which we'd all still be living in caves. Evolution means that if something helps us to survive, then our children and their children will share the same characteristic. Over time, the left side of the brain has become more developed. And that's what causes most people to be right-handed.

2 Wink. Which eye did you use?

3 Pick up the tube and look through it. Which eye did you use?

4 Take a drink. Which hand did you use to pick up the cup?

5 Throw the ball. Which hand feels most natural to use?

6 Run and then take a jump. Which leg did you use to kick off?

7 Kick the ball along the ground. Which foot did you use?

RIGHT	LEFT
✓	✓
✓	
✓	
✓	

8 At the end of the experiments, see how many check marks there are in each column. Chances are they'll all be in one column—probably the right-hand one.

In the Real World
Ninety percent of the world's population are right-handed, while about 80 percent are right-footed and 70 percent are right-eye-dominant. In the past, teachers would try to force children to write with their right hand, even if they were left-handed, because it was considered to be a disadvantage. Now it's believed this would hinder a child's natural development.

Take it Further Make a circle with your index finger and thumb. Find an object on the opposite wall and center it inside your finger-thumb circle. Close your left eye. Then open it and close your right eye. If the object moves when you close your left eye, then your right is the dominant eye. If it moves when you close your right eye, the reverse is true. You may find that although you favor your right hand, arm, and leg, that your left eye is actually dominant. This is fairly common.

TAP 'N' FREEZE

Here's how to freeze a plastic bottle of water just by tapping it.

You Will Need
- bottled water (distilled or filtered is best, but do not use mineral water)
- freezer
- watch or phone with timer

1 Lay the bottle of water down in the freezer compartment.

2 You need to wait until the bottle is very cold but the water is still liquid. How long the water takes to get to the right temperature depends on how big the bottle is, so keep checking back.

3 When you think the water's on the verge of freezing, take out the bottle and tap it on the table.

4 If you've judged it correctly, the water in the bottle will freeze before your very eyes. If it doesn't, put it back in the freezer and try again in a few minutes. This may happen a few times. When you're successful, make a note of how long it took.

What's the Science?

Tap water freezes at 32° Fahrenheit because it has tiny particles and other impurities in it. These help the crystallization process which forms ice. The bottled water doesn't have these, so it can stay liquid at a lower temperature. But when you tap the bottle on the table, the energy released kicks off a process called nucleation. A single crystal forms, which quickly starts a chain reaction to form other crystals—and the bottle will freeze before your eyes.

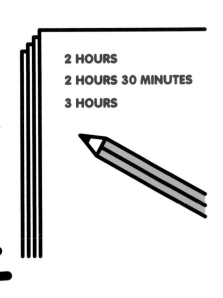

2 HOURS
2 HOURS 30 MINUTES
3 HOURS

THE IMPOSSIBLE PLANE

Paper planes need to look sleek and aerodynamic to fly properly... don't they? Apparently not!

You Will Need

- plastic drinking straw
- some stiff cardboard
- scissors
- tape

1 Cut the cardboard into two strips about 1 inch wide. One strip should be twice as long as the other.

2 Bend the longer strip to form a circle and secure the ends with the tape (make sure the ends overlap a bit). Do the same with the shorter strip.

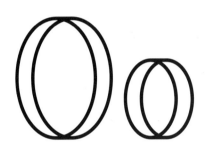

3 Tape the hoops to the straw, as shown. The larger one goes at the back and the smaller one at the front. You'll find that this bizarrely shaped plane will fly further than a traditional one.

What's the Science?

The hoop at the back creates air resistance—known as drag—and the smaller one at the front prevents the plane from turning so it stays on course, helping it to fly further.

PINECONE WEATHER STATION

Nature's really good at predicting the weather, as this simple experiment demonstrates.

You Will Need
- some pinecones
- pencil and paper to record weather forecasts
- modeling clay

3 If they open up, then the weather will be dry. (You may need to wait several hours before seeing a change.)

2 If the cones close up, this tells you that it's going to rain.

1 Place the pinecones on a flat surface outside. Use the modeling clay to make sure they stay upright.

4 Record the weather forecasts on the paper and see if they come true.

What's the Science?

Inside a cone are tiny, tiny seeds. When it's dry, the cone opens so that the seeds can be carried away by the wind. Eventually they'll fall on the ground to sprout and turn into pine trees. When the air gets more humid, it's usually a sign that it's going to rain, so the pinecones close to protect the seeds from getting wet, because wet seeds aren't blown as far by the wind.

BLOW IN THE BOTTLE TRICK

Bet your friends that they can't blow a paper ball into an empty bottle. You'll win every time.

You Will Need
- empty plastic bottle
- ball of crumpled paper

1 Crumple the paper so that it just fits inside the neck of the bottle.

2 Get one of your friends to blow it into the bottle with a single sharp breath.

3 Instead of going into the bottle, the paper will "bounce" back out.

What's the Science?

Although the bottle appears to be empty, it's actually full of air. When you blow against the paper, your breath flows around it and into the bottle to create pressure, which is enough to force the paper ball out again.

Take it Further You'd think that using a straw to concentrate your breath on the paper ball would do the trick, but it doesn't. Try it! The paper ball may wobble a little, but then it'll pop back out again.

THE AIR-POWERED CRANE

This is what's called a pneumatic machine—one that is powered by compressed air. Here's how to build one.

You Will Need
- 9 ordinary wooden craft sticks (a bit like popsicle sticks)
- 5 large craft sticks (about twice as wide)
- masking tape
- 2 plastic measuring syringes (no needle); 20 ml size should be fine (available online).
- all purpose glue
- some flexible plastic tubing (the same size as the ends of each syringe)

1 Start by making a triangle using three of the ordinary craft sticks and some tape to secure them.

2 Make a second triangle.

3 Link the two triangles together using the last three craft sticks and the tape. This shape will provide the stability you need.

4 Tape one of the larger craft sticks to the front sloping edge of the structure. It doesn't matter if it sticks out above the top.

5 Take a second large stick and tape this to the top of the first large craft stick. The trick here is to leave enough of a gap between the two sticks so that the tape acts as a hinge.

6 Take one of the syringes and glue the end of the plunger (where you would put your thumb) to the underside (nearest the frame) of the larger craft stick you just attached.

7 Make sure the plunger is fully pushed in, then tape one end of the plastic tubing to the nozzle of the syringe.

8 Tape the nozzle and tubing to the bottom of your contraption.

9 Take the second syringe and pull the plunger out to fill it full of air. Attach it to the other end of the tubing with tape.

10 Depress the plunger of the second syringe. This will push out the plunger of the first syringe and cause the hinged craft stick to rise.

11 Add another large craft stick to the end of the raised stick to extend the reach of your crane.

What's the Science?

It's all about controlling the flow of the air that's compressed in the syringes. By making a seal between the two syringes, the air can't escape. As it's pushed from one syringe to another, it generates the lift required to raise the crane.

Take it Further Try wrapping a paper clip around the end of your crane to form a hook, or glue on a magnet so you can pick up metal objects. For more power, try replacing the air in the syringes with water.

SALT BEGONE!

In this simple experiment, we'll show you how to remove salt from salt water without even touching it.

You Will Need
- three cups of water
- small bowl
- larger bowl
(about three times the size)
- plastic wrap
- small stone
- 1 1/2 tablespoons of salt

1 Pour three cups of water into the larger bowl and stir in the salt.

2 Place the empty small bowl into the larger bowl (don't let any salt water get into it).

3 Cover the larger bowl with plastic wrap, sealing it all around the edge.

4 Place the stone in the center of the plastic wrap so that its weight pushes the wrap down slightly, toward the small bowl.

5 Carefully put the whole thing out into the sunshine and wait about an hour.

6 Fresh water will collect under the plastic wrap and drip into the small bowl. Taste it and see!

What's the Science?

The sun's heat evaporates the salt water. Pure water molecules evaporate into the air, leaving the salt behind, until they hit the plastic wrap. They condense there to form droplets. These roll down the plastic and drip into the small bowl—and you have fresh water!

DISTANT THUNDER

It's easy to tell when a thunderstorm is likely to hit. All you need to do is count!

You Will Need
- a thunderstorm, somewhere in the distance
- your brain

1 Watch for a lightning strike.

2 When you see it, start counting (one-Mississippi, two-Mississippi style).

In the Real World

Although some people are afraid of thunder, the sound of it can't hurt you. But thunder is the sound of lightning, and anywhere between 6,000 and 24,000 people are killed by lightning every year. (The reason we don't know the exact number is because many countries where lightning storms are common don't keep good records.)

3 How long until you hear the thunder? For every five seconds that it takes, the storm is one mile away. When there's no gap between lightning and thunder, the storm is overhead.

What's the Science?

Light travels faster than sound. Lightning and thunder actually occur at the same time, but you see the light almost instantly, while the sound takes longer to reach you. That's because light travels incredibly fast, at more than 186,000 miles per second. By contrast, sound "crawls" along at about one-fifth of a mile per second.

FLOATING M&MS

Candy may taste good, but did you know that it is also useful for science experiments? Here's a neat trick you can do with some water and one of your favourite types of candy.

You Will Need
- bowl
- some water
- handful of M&Ms

1 Put the M&Ms in the bowl with the labels facing up.

2 Carefully add the water (try to pour it around the M&Ms so you don't disturb them too much).

3 Wait for 5 to 10 minutes then look again. The labels should have mysteriously lifted off the M&Ms.

WOW!

What's the Science?
The colored coating on the M&Ms is soluble, meaning that it dissolves in water. However, the edible paper that the "m" is printed on is not. So, when the hard candy shell has dissolved, the "m" lifts off and floats to the surface.

FAT FINGERS

Have you ever wondered how some animals stay comfortable in freezing weather? Here's how they do it.

You Will Need
- two bowls with water in them
- ice cubes
- some white fat (sometimes called lard)

1 Add the ice cubes to both bowls of water and let them get nice and cold.

2 Press or roll the fat out so it forms a square about the length of one finger.

3 Wrap the fat around the index finger of one hand, making sure it also covers the tip.

4 Put that finger and your other index finger into the two bowls of water.

5 Pretty soon the finger without the fat will get so cold that you can't keep it in the water any more. But how does the other one feel?

What's the Science?

The fat is a poor conductor of heat, which means it keeps out the cold in the icy water. At the same time, it keeps in the natural warmth in your finger.

In the Real World

A whale's body temperature is pretty close to a human's —between 97 and 100 degrees Fahrenheit. Whales often swim in very cold water, so they have a layer of fat or blubber under their skin that keeps them warm. It can be between 6 and 24 inches thick, depending on the season.

THE 1970S LAVA LAMP

Back in the 1970s, everyone had one of these lamps that produced craaaaazy psychedelic effects. Here's how to make your own.

You Will Need

- clear, empty 1-liter soda bottle
- plastic funnel
- half a cup of water
- bottle of vegetable oil
- liquid food coloring
- one or two effervescent tablets (people take these for headaches with an upset stomach)

1 Put the funnel into the top of the bottle and add the water.

2 Pour in the vegetable oil until the bottle is nearly full.

3 Wait for the water and oil to separate (see What's the Science?).

In the Real World

When a tanker runs aground and spills its oil into the sea, the oil floats on top because it isn't as dense as the water.

4 Add about 10 drops of food coloring and wait until it falls through the oil to the water at the bottom.

5 Break one of the effervescent tablets into small pieces and drop one into the bottle.

6 As the tablet starts to fizz, bubbles of colored water will begin to rise up through the oil.

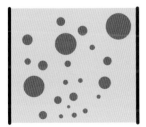

7 Dim the lights and shine a flashlight into the bottle from the side.

8 When the bubbling stops, add more fizz to re-start the show.

9 For an even fancier lava lamp effect, add some glitter into the mix—this will add a sparkling, star-like shimmer.

Take it Further If you have a glass table, make your lamp look even more fantastic by placing it on the top and shining a powerful flashlight from underneath. Turn the lights off for a spectacular show!

What's the Science?

Oil and water don't mix because the molecules that make up each one are more attracted to each other than they are to the molecules in the other substance. Oil is more viscous than water, but it isn't as dense—so it "floats" above the water. The food coloring is water-based, so it sinks to the bottom. When you add the tablets they release bubbles of carbon dioxide and these give the colored water a piggyback ride to the surface. The bubbles burst, the gas escapes, and the colored water drifts back down to the bottom of the bottle again.

THE WOBBLY BROOMSTICK

In just 20 seconds you can make yourself so dizzy that you'll fall over. Every time.

1 Hold the broomstick by one end in front of you. It should stick straight up in the air above your head.

You Will Need
- broomstick, or any other kind of pole
- lots of nice, soft grass—because you will fall over!

2 Look at the top of the broomstick and spin around in a circle. Spin 10 times for mild dizziness, and 20 times for an extreme experience!

3 Now try and walk in a straight line. If you fall over, see if you can stand up at all!

What's the Science?

Your ears are in charge of helping you keep your balance, thanks to tiny hair cells. They wave back and forth in a liquid current and tell your brain "where you are" in 3D space. As you spin, these hairs all move in the same direction and when you stop suddenly, it takes them a while to sort themselves out again. That is why you stagger around for a few moments before you get your balance back.

BALLOON IN A BOTTLE

Blowing up a balloon is easy, right? Not when it's inside a bottle, it isn't!

1 Ask an adult to help you poke a small hole in the side of the bottle. It should be big enough to let air flow in and out, but small enough to cover with your finger.

You Will Need
- empty plastic bottle
- pair of scissors or something else to make a hole in the bottle
- balloon

2 Push the balloon into the top of the bottle and then stretch the neck of the balloon over the top.

3 Hold your finger over the hole in the side of the bottle and try to blow the balloon up. You can't do it, can you?

What's the Science?

Although the bottle looks empty, it's full of air. When you try to blow the balloon up with your finger covering the hole, the air has nowhere to go, so the balloon doesn't inflate. If you uncover the hole, when you blow up the balloon you push the air in the bottle out of the hole. This makes room for the inflated balloon.

4 Remove your finger and try again. The balloon is now easy to blow up.

THE BAKING SODA BOAT

Yes, it's time to make your own powerboat!

You Will Need

- small empty water bottle with a lid
- something to poke a hole in the top
- plastic straw
- blob of adhesive putty
- 1 1/2 cups of vinegar
- 1 tablespoon of baking soda
- bathtub with water in it

1 Ask an adult to help you poke a hole in the bottle top, just big enough for the straw to fit through.

2 Cut the straw in half and push it into the hole you just made. It should stick out the top by an inch or two.

3 Use the putty to secure the straw inside and outside the bottle top.

4 Pour the vinegar into the bottle.

5 Add the baking soda, then quickly screw the top of the bottle back on and lay it flat in the bathtub.

6 Off goes your powerboat!

What's the Science?

Vinegar is an acid and baking soda is a base. When you mix them together, they neutralize each other and release carbon dioxide. This is expelled out of the straw to create bubbles in the water, and this pushes the boat along.

THE RAINMAKER

This simple experiment demonstrates how rain is formed. You'll need an adult to help with this.

You Will Need
- saucepan full of water
- metal tray
- plenty of ice cubes
- oven mitts

1 Ask an adult to help you boil the water in the saucepan.

3 Use the oven mitts to hold the tray of ice above the pan of boiling water.

2 Pour the ice cubes onto the metal tray.

In the Real World
This is exactly how rain is formed. The sun evaporates water, which rises as vapor before condensing to form clouds and, eventually, rain.

4 Watch as drops form quickly under the tray before falling back into the pan as "rain."

What's the Science?
The surface of the metal tray remains cold, thanks to the ice cubes. As steam rises from the boiling water, it condenses on the underside of the tray to form droplets of water. They drip back into the pan as "rain."

MAKE YOUR OWN ICE CREAM

It's the one we've all been waiting for—the recipe for making your very own delicious ice cream. Yay!

You Will Need
- 2 re-sealable quart-size freezer bags
- 1 re-sealable gallon-size freezer bag
- 1/2 cup milk
- 1/2 teaspoon vanilla flavoring
- 1 tablespoon sugar
- 4 cups of crushed ice
- 4 tablespoons of salt (yes, salt!)
- gloves

What's the Science?

The ice cubes surrounding the ice cream mixture reduce the temperature, but the real key is the addition of the salt. Adding salt to ice lowers the temperature at which it freezes, making the surrounding bag of melting ice incredibly cold—cold enough to turn the mixture inside the inner bags into ice cream. Without the addition of salt, the temperature would not drop low enough to make ice cream and the ingredients would stay all slushy. No ice cream for you!

1 Mix the milk, vanilla, and sugar together in one of the quart-sized bags.

2 When they're mixed, squeeze as much air out of the bag as you can and seal it.

3 Place the sealed bag inside the other quart-sized bag.

4 Again, squeeze as much air out of that bag as you can and seal that.

5 Place the sealed quart-sized bags inside the gallon-sized bag.

6 Fill this bag with ice and sprinkle the salt on top of the ice.

7 Squeeze the air out as much as you can and seal this bag as well.

8 Put your gloves on and shake the bag to ensure that the ice completely surrounds the two smaller bags inside.

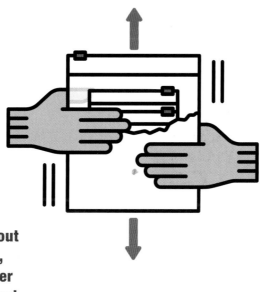

Take it Further Not a fan of vanilla ice cream? Want something a bit more exciting? Add chocolate chips or crushed candy, nuts, or chocolate syrup.

9 Keep shaking. After about seven or eight minutes, you'll be able to tell whether the mixture is starting to feel like ice cream. When it does, open all the bags and grab your spoon!

In the Real World

When an ice cream vendor ran out of dishes to serve his customers at the St. Louis World's Fair in 1904, the guy next door came to the rescue, thanks to the crisp pastry (a little like a waffle) that he was selling. Together they produced the first ice cream cone.

VANISHING TRICK

How easy is it to make something disappear? With the help of science, it turns out to be pretty easy...

You Will Need
- large Pyrex beaker (large enough to drop a test tube into)
- Pyrex test tube
- vegetable oil

1 Take the test tube and hold it in the beaker. It's clearly visible, right?

2 Remove the test tube and fill the beaker with vegetable oil.

What's the Science?

Usually light reflects off an object and that's how we can see it. But when light moves between mediums (that's a fancy word for different kinds of "stuff" like oil and air) it changes speed. Although some of the light is still reflected, some of it is refracted—it bends around corners. By coincidence, Pyrex and vegetable oil have the same refractive index. That means light travels at exactly the same speed through both of them. Put them together and the light is neither reflected nor refracted. The Pyrex test tube becomes "invisible," even though you know it's there!

WOW!

3 Lower the test tube into the beaker until it's covered by the oil. As you do, watch it disappear before your eyes!

HOW MANY CUBES?

How is it possible to look at the same set of cubes in a drawing and see different numbers of squares each time?

1 You could just use the drawing on this page, but to get the full effect, copy out the shape for yourself.

2 Color in each side of your square with one of your three favourite colors, following the pattern in the drawing.

You Will Need
- pencil
- ruler
- crayons
- sheet of paper

3 The first time you look at the drawing, focus on Starting Point 1 and count the number of cubes. There are seven.

4 Then look at Starting Point 2 and do the same. This time there are only six.

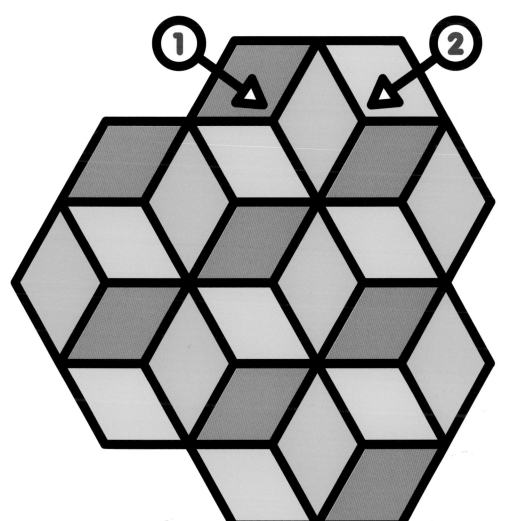

What's the Science?

This is a two-dimensional drawing, so it has width and height. Because of the way it's drawn, your brain wants to turn it into something that has three dimensions—width, height, and depth. Depending on where your eye "falls," you might see two cubes on the top row first and go on to count seven in total. Or maybe you'll see a single square first and go on to count six.

MY BAG WON'T LEAK!

When you poke a hole in a bagful of water, you'd expect the water to come rushing out, right? Maybe not...

1 Pour some water into the bag.

2 Seal the top of the bag.

You Will Need
- sealable plastic bag
- sharp pencil
- water
- some outside space where it doesn't matter if you spill water

3 Get a grown-up to hold the bag while you poke a hole in it with the pencil. Push the pencil all the way through and out the other side. Do this very quickly—don't worry if you need a couple of attempts.

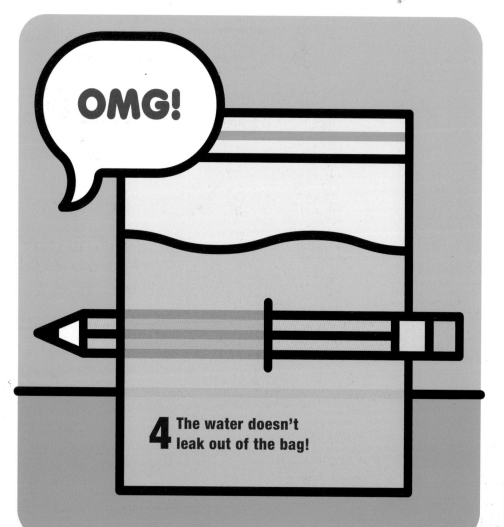

OMG!

4 The water doesn't leak out of the bag!

What's the Science?

The plastic in the bag is constructed from polymers. ("Poly" means "many" and "mer" means "part.") Polymers are special because they're made from long, flexible chains of molecules. When the pencil point pierces the bag, the polymers expand to make a seal around the pencil and keep the water from escaping.

INVISIBLE INK

This simple experiment is perfect if you want to write secret messages to your friends.

You Will Need

- half a lemon
- bowl
- spoon
- water
- cotton swab
- white paper
- lamp with a bare light bulb

1 Squeeze juice from the lemon into the bowl. Remove any seeds.

2 Stir in a few drops of water.

3 Dip the cotton swab into the "ink."

4 Write your message on the paper. Make it a good one!

What's the Science?

Lemon juice contains carbon compounds which are colorless. But when you apply heat, they oxidize and turn brown—which is why you can see the message when you hold it over the light bulb.

5 When it's dry, give your message to a friend. To read it, tell them to get a grown-up to hold the paper over an incandescent light bulb. All will be revealed!

In the Real World

You can see another example of this if you leave your lemon on a windowsill in the sun. It will turn brown because of oxidation.

MAKE A WATERWHEEL

Before steam and electricity, water was used as a power source. This simple machine shows you how to use it to lift a heavy metal washer.

You Will Need
- **empty plastic spool (from cotton thread or tape)**
- **disposable plastic cup**
- **plastic drinking straw**
- **duct tape**
- **fishing line or dental floss**
- **heavy metal washer**
- **empty 2-liter soda bottle**
- **scissors and a utility knife**

1 If the plastic cup has a lip, ask an adult to cut it off.

2 Measure about an inch down from the top of the cup and cut a strip all the way around, so you have a circle of plastic.

3 Check the height of the spool, then cut the circle of plastic into six rectangles that are the same height.

4 Tape these six "blades" to your empty spool, making sure they're evenly spaced. This is your waterwheel.

5 Poke the straw through the hole in the middle of the empty spool and tape it in place.

In the Real World
Waterwheels were used for hundreds of years. Millers used them to grind flour to make bread. Some ground wood into pulp to make paper.

6 Get a grown-up to cut off the top of the soda bottle to leave you with a tall, free-standing "tank."

7 Now ask them to cut a couple of v-shaped notches in the top of the bottle for the straw to rest on.

8 Poke half a dozen holes in the sides near the bottom of the bottle (so water can drain away).

9 Wrap some tape around one end of the straw and then tie the fishing line (or dental floss) around that section of tape. Make the line slightly longer than the bottle is tall.

10 Tie the other end of the line around the heavy washer.

11 Lay the water wheel (empty spool and straw) across the top of the bottle.

12 Put the bottle in the sink under the fauced. Turn the water on—gently—and watch what happens!

What's the Science?

It's pure engineering. As the water from the fauced hits the blades, it pushes them down and the wheel begins to turn. As the wheel turns, the line or thread is wrapped around the straw, lifting the heavy washer up into the air.

THE MAZY PLANT

Here's how to "train" a plant so that it grows through a maze.

You Will Need
- shoebox
- some cardboard
- scissors
- clear tape
- houseplant

1 Cut a hole in one end of the shoebox. It should be about 1 to 1 1/2 inches across.

2 Cut some of the cardboard to make two or three "half walls" to fit inside the box. The walls should only go about halfway across the width of the box.

3 Fix the half walls into position with the tape, staggering them by starting on one side of the box, then the other, then back to the other side.

4 Water the plant and then place it in the box at the opposite end from the hole.

5 Put the lid on the box and place it on its end in a sunny place.

6 It may take four or five days, but eventually your plant will emerge through the hole.

What's the Science?

This happens because plants need sunlight in order to thrive, so they will naturally grow toward a light source —in this case, the light coming in through the hole in the shoebox. This "growing toward the light" is called phototropism.

TURN A PENNY GREEN

This simple experiment will demonstrate how to turn a coin from bronze to green.

You Will Need
- penny
- some white vinegar
- bowl
- piece of paper towel

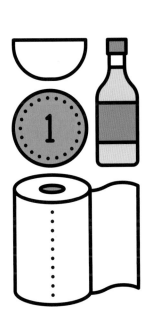

1 Put the paper towel in the bowl and place your penny on top.

2 Carefully, pour the vinegar over the penny and paper towel so that the paper towel is soaked.

3 Leave it for a couple of days, then flip the penny over and add more vinegar.

In the Real World
The Statue of Liberty in New York is covered in a layer of copper. This combines with air (and pollution) to form malachite, which is why it has that distinctive green coloring.

What's the Science?
The penny turns green because it's made of copper. When you add vinegar, this reacts with the air to produce a greeny-blue compound called malachite, which coats the penny.

WOW!

4 Watch as the penny magically turns green!

THE TUNEFUL TUBE

This simple experiment lets you make music with just an ordinary plastic tube.

You Will Need
- flexible plastic tubing, about 3 feet long (get the kind with ridges inside, sometimes called conduit tubing)
- plastic bag (optional)
- tape (optional)

1 Hold one end of the tube and start to whirl it around and around.

2 When it reaches a particular speed you'll hear a note.

What's the Science?

The far end of the tube moves faster than the end you're holding, so the air pressure there is lower. Air always moves from high to low pressure, so it rushes through the tube. This is where the ridges come in! Air molecules bounce off the ridges to create tiny vortices (like mini whirlwinds) that vibrate at the natural frequency of the tube. When you cover the end with a bag filled with air, the sound stops when the air runs out. No air = no sound.

3 Try whirling the tube faster and slower and see if you can change the note.

Take it Further Tape the plastic bag to one end of the tube, then blow into the other end to inflate the bag. Now, holding the tube at the bag end, whirl it around. You'll hear a note and then, as the air is sucked from the bag, the note will fade away.

WHAT A JERK!

Let's find out why it's impossible to keep your leg still when someone gives it a tap just below the knee.

You Will Need
- a chair to sit on
- your hand

1 Sit down on the chair and cross your legs so that the top one can swing freely over the bottom one.

2 Give yourself a firm tap just below the knee of the top leg. Use the side of your hand, like a karate chop.

What's the Science?

When you stand, your muscles are stretching and contracting all the time; this keeps you from falling over. The tendon below your knee (which is what you're tapping) is connected to the big muscle along the top of your thigh. As you tap the tendon, it stretches the muscle, which then contracts immediately to counteract the stretch and keep you balanced. But because you're sitting down, your lower leg actually kicks up in the air as a result.

3 Your lower leg will kick out, whether you want it to or not.

THE ELECTRIC LEMON

Did you know that you can use a lemon to make enough electricity to power a small light bulb? Well, you do now!

You will need

- four lemons
- four pennies
- four galvanized nails (sometimes called corrosion-resistant nails)
- five alligator clip cables
- LED light (the kind with two little wires coming out of the bottom)
- knife

1 Ask an adult to cut a penny-sized slit into a lemon with the knife.

2 Stick a nail and a penny into the lemon so they stick out, as shown in the illustration. It's important not to let the nail and penny touch.

3 Repeat Steps 1 and 2 for the other three lemons.

4 Line up your lemons. Clip one end of an alligator cable onto the nail on the lemon that's furthest left.

5 Take a second alligator cable and attach it to the penny on the lemon that's furthest right.

6 Now, chain the lemons together using the remaining alligator cables in sequence. It should go penny to nail, penny to nail, penny to nail.

7 You should now have all the lemons connected, with a spare clip at each end.

8 Find the spare clip that is connected to the nail at the other end and attach it to the shorter of the two little wires coming out of the light. This is the negative connection.

9 Attach the other spare clip to the longer wire on the light (you guessed it, this is the positive connection).

10 On comes the light, powered only by lemons!

What's the Science?

All batteries (whether you buy them at the store or make them out of lemons) work the same way—they contain chemicals that react with each other to create electricity when the electrons inside the battery are allowed to flow freely between the negative terminal and the positive one. This is exactly what happens when you clip the two free cables to the negative and positive wires on the LED bulb, to complete the circuit. In this experiment, the nails are the negative terminals and the pennies are the positive ones. Each lemon, coin, and nail only generate about one volt of electricity, which is why we need four to light up the LED bulb.

PETRIFIED PEPPER

**Pepper, huh? Thinks it's tough...
not scared of anything, right?
Well, let's just see...**

1 Sprinkle the pepper over the water so that it lightly covers the entire surface (or most of it, at least).

2 Dip one end of the toothpick into the dishwashing liquid.

You Will Need
- a bowl half-filled with water
- ground pepper (out of a shaker)
- wooden toothpick
- dishwashing liquid

3 Very carefully, touch the tip that has dishwashing liquid on it onto the water (right in the middle is best).

4 The pepper shoots away from the toothpick as if terrified!

What's the Science?

Water molecules are very strongly attracted to each other, and this creates something called surface tension. Adding a drop of dishwashing liquid breaks that surface tension, but the water molecules keep being attracted to each other. Since they can't "compete" with the dishwashing liquid, they pull away from it and toward each other, taking the specks of pepper with them.

HELP!

Take it Further You can see surface tension in action when you overfill a glass of water. It literally bulges over the top of the glass.

WHY YOU SHOULD ALWAYS BRUSH YOUR TEETH

What does an egg have to do with brushing your teeth? Leave one in some cola overnight and you'll find out.

You Will Need
- **hard-boiled egg with a white shell**
- **glass**
- **cola**
- **toothbrush and toothpaste**

1 Get an adult to hard-boil an egg for you, then put it into the empty glass.

2 Fill the glass with cola and leave it overnight.

3 In the morning, pour the cola away.

4 The egg will have turned brown.

5 Brush the egg with toothpaste to clean the stains off.

What's the Science?

The shell of an egg is a lot like the shell around your teeth, which is called enamel. If you don't brush your teeth, then the dark brown compounds in the cola will be absorbed into the enamel. Your teeth will turn—and stay—brown.

DON'T GET SOAKED

Nobody likes to get wet...oh, who are we kidding? Everyone likes to get wet, which is why you'll hate this experiment.

1 Pour water into the bucket until it's about half full.

You Will Need
- **bucket with a strong handle**
- **some water**
- **outside space (in case things get messy)**

2 Stand in a clear, open space and start swinging the bucket in a circle in front of you, as if you were drawing a clock face with your arm.

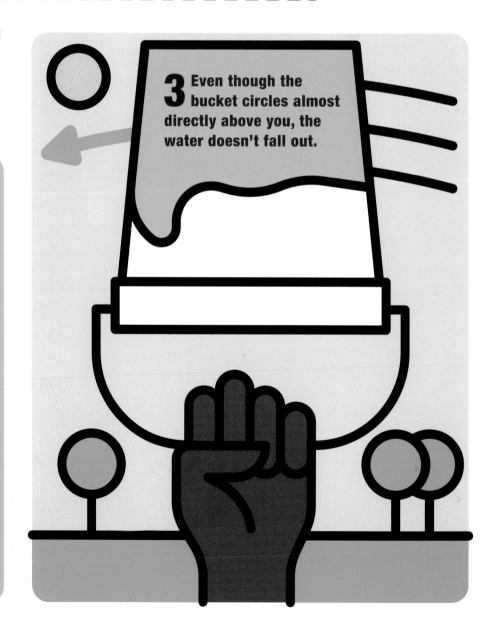

3 Even though the bucket circles almost directly above you, the water doesn't fall out.

What's the Science?

If you were to swing the bucket of water behind you, then in front of you and let go, both the bucket and the water inside it would fly away from you. However, because you keep swinging the bucket by the handle and don't let go, you're exerting what's called centripetal force—pulling the bucket of water toward an imaginary centre point. As long as you swing fast enough, the the water will always stay in the bucket, instead of falling on your head!

MAP THE SOLAR SYSTEM

This is a really fun experiment which will help you understand just how vast the solar system actually is.

1 Use the table on this page to draw circles that represent scale models of each planet, then cut them out.

Planet	Diameter in miles	Diameter in inches	Steps from the Sun
Mercury	3,032	0.2	1
Venus	7,521	0.5	2
Earth	7,926	0.5	3
Mars	4,222	0.25	4
Jupiter	88,846	5.6	13
Saturn	74,898	4.75	25
Uranus	31,763	2	50
Neptune	30,775	2	78

You Will Need
- **eight pieces of paper**
- **scissors**
- **sports field or park**
- **eight friends**
- **pencil**

2 Write the name of the planet on each circle and hand them out to your friends.

JUPITER

3 Now head outside. You're the sun, so get each of your friends to move the right number of steps away from you (see table) and you'll get a sense of how enormous the solar system is.

What's the Science?

Since we can't actually get the person holding Neptune to walk 2.8 billion miles away, we have to use a scale—where one small measurement represents a much bigger measurement. In this case we've decided that one step equals 36 million miles. Similarly, we can't draw circles that are 8,000 miles across, so we've taken the actual diameter of each planet in the solar system and divided it by 1,000,000,000 to end up with something small enough to hold in your hand!

THE POPSICLE BRIDGE

How can something made out of flimsy popsicle sticks hold up a heavy weight? It's all to do with triangles and design.

You Will Need
- about 100 popsicle sticks (you can use craft sticks from a hobby shop)
- glue
- glue gun (optional)
- cable ties
- scissors
- nylon cord
- fishing scale

1 Make a triangle from three craft sticks, like this.

2 Add a second triangle, carefully attaching the sticks at each corner with glue.

3 Keep going until you have seven triangles, arranged like this.

4 Strengthen the structure with additional crosspieces, as shown here.

5 Keep adding additional crosspieces until the structure looks like this.

6 Repeat Steps 1–5 to complete the other side of the bridge.

7 Now make the bottom section. Start with four craft sticks glued to make a square.

8 Add more squares until you have four in a row.

9 Add crosspieces to make the whole bottom section stronger.

10 Arrange the bottom and sides of the bridge to make a triangular shape, then secure the first corner with a cable tie.

11 Continue tying the parts of the bridge together with the ties as shown (you can snip off the ends of the cable ties to make it look neater).

12 Balance the bridge across a space—between two chairs, for example—and thread the nylon cord through the bridge, along the other side and back out through the bridge again toward you.

What's the Science?

It's all to do with the triangles! The triangle is incredibly important in engineering projects because it can't be bent or twisted without either breaking one of its joints or altering the length of one of its sides. Squares, on the other hand, are easy to bend and twist. That's why we cross the squares that make up the bottom of the bridge with additional sticks to turn them into triangles.

13 Tie a knot in the cord so you can hang the fishing scale from it.

14 Pull down on the scale (gently at first!) and see how much pressure you can exert. You may be able to pull as much as 50 pounds before the bridge starts to crack! Be careful not to fall over or get hit with the scale when the bridge breaks.

THE BALLOON AMPLIFIER

Balloons are really good at making noise sound louder. Here's how it works.

You Will Need
- a balloon
- your ears

1 Blow up the balloon as much as you can and tie off the end.

2 Tap the side of the balloon and listen to the sound it makes. Not very loud, is it?

3 Now place the inflated balloon next to your ear and tap it again. The sound you hear is much, much louder.

What's the Science?

The air around us is pretty good at conducting sound—that's how we hear stuff all the time. When you blow air into the balloon, you're forcing the air molecules closer together, which makes them an even better conductor of sound. So when you tap the other side of the balloon, the sound you hear is really loud.

THE VANISHING RAINBOW

How can you make something so colorful just disappear before your very eyes? It's simple, really.

You Will Need
- white cardboard
- cup or glass
- pencil
- scissors
- ruler
- felt-tip pens or crayons in six different colors
- string
- something to make holes in the cardboard

1 Turn the glass or cup over on the cardboard and draw around it with the pencil, then cut the circle out.

2 Use the pencil and ruler to divide the circle into six equal sections.

3 Color each section a different color: red, orange, yellow, green, blue, and purple.

4 Poke two small holes just to each side of the middle of the circle.

5 Cut two pieces of string about 24 inches long and thread one through each hole.

6 Tie them off at the ends.

7 Holding both ends of the string, whirl the wheel forward in a circle so the two pieces of string wind and twist around each other.

8 Spin the wheel really fast by pulling your hands apart to let the string unwind, then wind around itself again. The colors will vanish!

What's the Science?

White light isn't white at all—it's a mixture of all the colors of the spectrum. If you mix red, green, and blue lights, the result is white light. The same thing happens with the color wheel—the colors blend together and your eyes see a single, white circle. It's called additive color mixing.

SPARKS ARE FLYING

Here's how to create a simple device that will hold an electric charge—and give you a mild shock every time!

You Will Need
- **thick square of styrofoam (the kind that's used to pack electrical devices or sometimes used as insulation)**
- **woolen sock or glove**
- **disposable foil pie pan**
- **styrofoam cup**
- **tape**

1 Turn the styrofoam cup upside down and use the tape to stick it onto the pie pan.

2 Take your woolen glove or sock and use it to rub the styrofoam square vigorously for one minute. (If you don't rub for long enough, the experiment won't work very well.)

3 Next, pick the pie pan up by the cup and drop the whole thing onto the styrofoam square.

4 Bring your finger close to the edge of the pie pan—about half an inch should do the trick. Watch what happens!

5 You'll get a small electric shock and will actually see a spark jump from the pie pan to your finger.

6 Lift the pie pan off the styrofoam square again using the cup "handle" and then move your finger near the edge again. Yep, another shock!

7 You can repeat this two or three times before the charge eventually disappears.

What's the Science?

By rubbing the styrofoam with the woolen glove (or sock), you're giving it an excess negative charge. The foil pie pan has no excess charge, so when you drop it onto the negatively charged styrofoam square, the electrons in the foam repel the electrons on the pie pan. However, the electrons can't go anywhere because they're surrounded by foam underneath and air all around—both of which are insulators. When you bring your finger near the pie pan, the electrons are able to jump off the pan and onto you—ouch! Now the pie pan has a positive charge and if you bring your finger near it again, you'll get another small shock.

FIRE AND WATER

1 Remove the label from the water bottle.

Water's for putting out fires, right? Unless you can find a way of using it to start them...

You Will Need
- clear plastic bottle of water with a rounded top
- piece of black paper (or you could use your printer to print out a big black square)

2 Standing outside in the sun, ask an adult to hold out the sheet of paper. You're in charge of the water bottle. Hold it so that it is between the paper and the sun.

3 Experiment until you get the right angle and distance between the bottle and the paper. When you do, you can focus the sun's rays on the black square. You'll see it as a little circle of light.

What's the Science?
A bottle with a rounded top works best because it acts just like a magnifying glass. It increases the power of the sun's rays, making the beam of light hot enough to start a fire. Black absorbs light better than any other color, which helps the fire start more quickly. Try this experiment with plain white paper and you'll find it's much harder.

4 After a few moments, the paper will start to smolder and then catch on fire. Use the water in the bottle to put it out.

HANDS UP!

Most people think they have control over what their arms do, but sometimes, that's just not so.

You Will Need
- doorway you can stand in
- your arms

1 Stand in the doorframe.

2 Hold your arms by your sides with the palms facing toward you. Raise them until they touch the door frame.

3 Push out with your arms against the door frame for about one minute.

4 Put your arms back to your sides, step out of the door frame and relax.

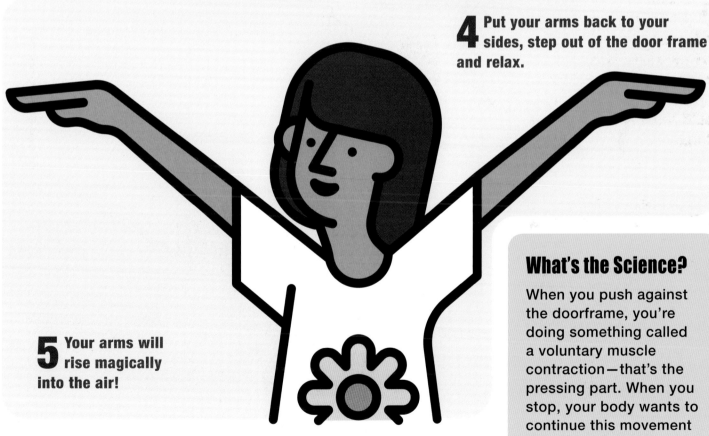

5 Your arms will rise magically into the air!

What's the Science?

When you push against the doorframe, you're doing something called a voluntary muscle contraction—that's the pressing part. When you stop, your body wants to continue this movement with an involuntary muscle contraction, which is why your arms want to lift up like wings!

Take it Further If you really concentrate, you can prevent your arms from lifting in the air. It will feel like an actual force is trying to lift them up!

MAKING ROCK CANDY

The best experiments are the ones where you end up with something you can eat. (So long as you brush your teeth afterward—remember page 67!)

You Will Need
- about three cups of sugar (remember what we said about your teeth!)
- food coloring
- wooden spoon
- one cup of water
- wooden toothpick
- glass jar (or a glass)
- big saucepan
- clothespins

1 Pour the cup of water into a saucepan and ask an adult to light the burner.

2 Add a cup of sugar. Warning: sugar solution will exceed 212 °F before it boils, so be very careful!

3 When that's dissolved in the water, add more sugar slowly until no more sugar will dissolve. You should be able to use nearly all three cups of sugar.

4 The water should look cloudy by now.

5 Take the saucepan off the heat and let it cool.

6 Dip your toothpicks about halfway into the sugary water.

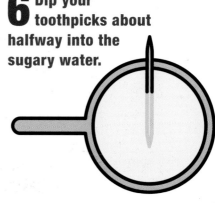

7 Roll the toothpicks in the remaining sugar to give them a light coating.

8 Leave them to dry (they must be completely dry or this won't work).

9 Fill the glass jar with the cooled sugar water.

10 Add a couple of drops of food coloring and stir it in.

11 Pinch the unsugared ends of the toothpicks in the clothespins, then lower them into the jar.

12 After a day, you'll start to see crystals forming on the toothpicks.

13 After three days, there should be a lot of crystals around your toothpicks.

14 At the end of the week, you'll have some crunchy rock candy to enjoy!

What's the Science?

You can only make so much sugar dissolve in the water when it's heated up—it's called a saturated solution. When it starts to cool down, it becomes a supersaturated solution—the water cannot hold all the sugar in solution, but the sugar needs something to form crystals on. It starts to crystallize on the tiny pieces of sugar on the toothpicks, which act as a sort of seed. The sugar crystals continue to grow on the toothpick until they form a tiny candy tree.

Take it Further You can prepare more glass jars and use different food coloring to produce many different kinds of colored candy.

THE BERNOULLI PRINCIPLE

We're nearing the end of the book so it's time for an experiment with a real scientific name!

1 Get your friend to see if they can blow up the plastic bag in five breaths.

You Will Need
- long, flimsy plastic bag (something like a trash bag will work)
- a friend

2 They'll probably be able to inflate about one third of the bag.

3 Now it's your turn! Instead of blowing the bag up like a balloon, hold it open on a flat surface in front of you.

4 Staying about 2 feet away from the open end of the bag, open it as much as you can and blow into it with a long steady breath.

5 As quickly as you can, seal the end and measure how much you were able to inflate the bag. It should be almost completely inflated!

What's the Science?

Daniel Bernoulli figured out that when you create a stream of air, the pressure around it drops. So blowing into the bag creates low pressure inside, and higher pressure from outside rushes into the bag to equalize the pressure. This air, combined with the air you're blowing into the bag, is enough to blow it up. When you blow the bag up like a balloon, this doesn't happen because you make a seal between the bag and your mouth.

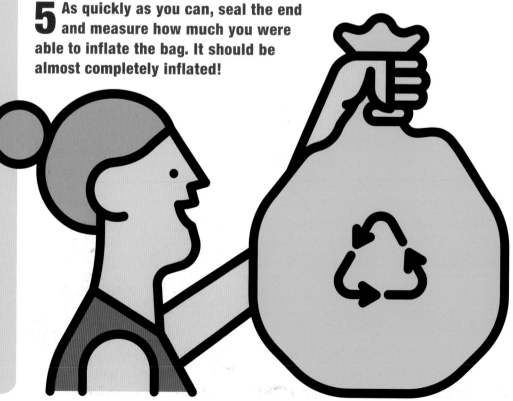

BONKERS BALLOONS

Let's see if we can make ordinary balloons behave in some strange ways!

1 Blow up the balloons.

You Will Need
- balloons
- a wall
- a clean, empty aluminum can

2 Rub them vigorously against a wool sweater, or your hair.

3 Touch a balloon against the wall—it should stick.

4 Take the two balloons and try to touch them together. It's harder than it looks!

5 Lay the can flat on its side on a table and then bring one of the balloons close to it. The can will roll toward the balloon.

What's the Science?

Rubbing the balloons against the wool or hair gives them a negative charge. They attract uncharged objects such as the can or the wall, in a way that's similar to a magnet attracting iron or steel. When you bring the two balloons together, they push against each other because they're both negatively charged.

WORMAPALOOZA!

Worms are secretive little creatures and we don't often get the chance to spy on their everyday life. Now you can!

You Will Need
- big glass jar (the bigger the better)
- empty aluminum can
- hammer and a nail
- sand and dirt
- potting soil
- water
- dry dog food
- worms (get these from the backyard or local bait shop)
- thick dark paper
- tape

1 Put the empty aluminum can in the bottom of the jar.

2 Add a layer of sand (1/2–1 inch deep) around it.

3 Add a layer of dirt the same depth on top of that.

4 Keep alternating sand and dirt until the jar is almost full (it works best if the top layer is dirt).

5 Put some worms on top.

6 Ask an adult to help you smash the dog food with the hammer.

7 Sprinkle it on top and then cover with potting soil. The jar should now be full.

What's the Science?

Placing the aluminum can in the jar forces the worms toward the sides when they make their tunnels, so we can see them. The worms dig tunnels by "eating" soil. They remove all the useful materials and then poop the rest (together with a good helping of worm "spit") out the back!

8 Add enough water to make the whole thing damp and moist, but not swimming in water.

9 Ask an adult to hammer some air holes in the metal lid of the jar.

10 Screw on the lid, then tape the dark paper around the jar. Put the whole thing somewhere safe—maybe on a shelf.

11 Every day or so, check to make sure the soil is moist. Add more water if you need to.

12 Every couple of weeks, add a bit more smashed-up dry dog food.

13 After the first week, you'll see that the worms have begun to construct a series of tunnels in the jar—something we'd never normally be able to see. (Don't forget to release the worms into the backyard when you have finished with them!)

In the Real World

As worms dig tunnels they aerate the soil, which allows air and water to pass through it more easily. This makes the kind of soil that plants love, which is why gardeners say that worms are their best friends!

THE SPOOL TANK

Here's how to make your own miniature tank, powered by a rubber band.

1 Ask an adult to cut a slice off the candle to make a disk.

You Will Need

- empty spool
- two matchsticks
- candle
- sharp knife
- something that can poke a hole in wax
- rubber band

2 Break one of the matches in half and throw away the end with the striker on it. Then snap the striker off the very end of the other match.

3 Poke a hole through the center of the candle slice.

4 Thread the rubber band through this hole, then through the center of the spool and out the other side.

5 Take the shorter piece of matchstick. Thread it through the loop at the end of the rubber band, on the side without the wax disk.

What's the Science?

As you twist the rubber band, you transfer energy to it. When you stop twisting the rubber band, this energy is released as the band untwists. Neither matchstick can turn—the longer one is pressed against the ground and the other one is held against the spool. So the spool itself turns and the "tank" rolls along.

6 Pull the other end of the rubber band and poke the longer piece of match through the loop at that end.

7 Twist the longer piece of match around and around to wind the rubber band up tight.

8 When you can't wind any more, put your tank on a flat surface and watch it go!

THE DISAPPEARING FACE

You never liked the look of that friend's face anyway, now did you?

You Will Need
- white wall
- square or rectangular mirror (small enough to hold in your hand)
- a friend
- two chairs

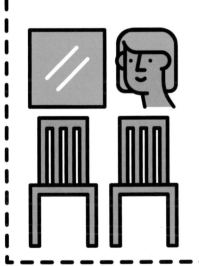

1 You and your friend should sit very still on the chairs facing each other, about 3 feet apart. The white wall is on your right and your friend's left.

2 Hold the mirror in your left hand so that the left edge is against the point of your nose and the mirror is angled at 45 degrees. Your right eye can only see a reflection of the white wall, while your left eye sees your friend's face.

3 Take your right hand and rub it across the white wall. You'll see parts of your friend's face vanish into thin air!

OMG!

What's the Science?

Normally your eyes each see a slightly different version of the same thing—your brain puts them together to form a 3D image. Here your eyes are seeing two very different things, but as long as you don't move, your brain can keep them separate. It's very sensitive to movement, so if you and your friend are very still, it will favor what your right eye sees when you move your hand. That's why it looks like you're "erasing" your friend's face.

IRON IN YOUR CEREAL!

They say a healthy breakfast cereal is rich in iron, but is it? Grab some cereal and we'll show you exactly how much iron you're eating every day!

You Will Need
- a bowl of cereal such as cornflakes (check the box to make sure it says it includes iron!)
- large glass bowl
- potato masher (or other tool) to mash up the cereal
- cup of hot water from the faucet
- spoon
- re-sealable freezer bag
- strong, flat magnet (a neodymium magnet will work best)

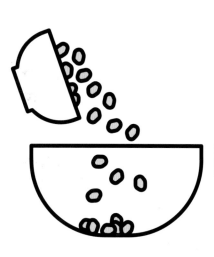

1 Pour out a bowl of dry cereal and tip it into the glass bowl.

2 Mash the cereal to a powder (it's fine if there are still a few larger pieces).

3 Add the water—just enough so that the cereal dissolves to form a sort of soup.

4 Carefully pour the "soup" into the re-sealable freezer bag.

5 Squeeze the air out of the bag and seal it.

6 Lay the bag on a table or other flat surface. The bag should lie flat.

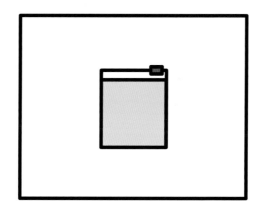

7 Slowly run the magnet across the surface of the bag. Start at one end and push toward the other end.

8 Repeat this motion until you start to see tiny specks of dark material along the edge you've been pushing toward.

9 Run the magnet slowly along the same edge from left to right and you'll attract all the tiny specks to the magnet.

In the Real World

Why do we need iron? It helps make red blood cells, which are necessary for moving oxygen around the body efficiently. If you don't have enough iron you can become anaemic—you'll look pale and get tired and short of breath more easily.

What's the Science?

When your cereal says it's "fortified with iron," it really is—but it's broken down into such tiny pieces that you can't see it. By crushing the cereal and then adding water, we can free the iron and then use magnetic attraction to bring it all together so you can see it.

10 At the end you'll see a surprising amount of what is clearly iron!

THE IMPOSSIBLE SIGNATURE

You remember how to write your own name, right? Not when you try doing it this way, you won't!

1 Sit at the table with the paper in front of you.

You Will Need
- piece of paper
- pencil
- chair and table

2 Lift your right foot and start moving it in a circle, clockwise.

3 Take the pencil and try to write your name. It doesn't matter whether you do it as a signature or just printing.

What's the Science?

Your brain and your body "talk" to each other all the time—they're having a constant conversation! Scientists believe that some parts of this conversation are more important than others. In this experiment, your brain pays more attention to what your hand is doing because it considers your hand to be "dominant." When you start writing, your foot begins to follow the path of your signature.

4 No matter how hard you try to prevent it, your foot will start to follow the "path" of your signature!

GROW YOUR OWN NAME

This is a really cool way to "sign" your name so everyone can see it.

1 Lay the cotton out on a flat surface.

You Will Need
- large square of cotton
- some cress seeds
- spray bottle
- stencil made from cardboard (optional)

2 If you're using a stencil, draw your name on the cardboard and then get an adult to help you cut out the shape of each letter.

3 Either sprinkle the seeds in the shape of your name, or lay the stencil on the cotton and sprinkle the seeds into the gaps that make up each letter.

4 Remove the stencil (if you've used it) and give the whole cotton square a good spray of water.

5 Keep the cotton moist and in a few days you'll start to see your name growing out of the cotton!

What's the Science?

Many seeds do not need soil to germinate. All that cress seeds need is air, light, and water. The cotton doesn't do anything except provide a store of water and a surface for the seeds' roots to hang onto. The rest is achieved by photosynthesis, the process in which plants take the light from the sun and turn it into chemical energy for growth.

MAKE A MINIATURE ROBOT

It's time to build your own moving robot with just a few simple household items and a couple of cheap electronic components.

You Will Need
- old plastic hairbrush with a rectangular head
- round mini electric motor with a red and a black wire coming out of it (it should be a 9 to 12 volt motor)
- on/off slide switch with two connectors (sometimes called an **SPST** switch)
- short screw
- 9-volt battery
- small hacksaw
- wire cutters or sharp scissors
- glue gun

1 Get an adult to saw the handle off the plastic hairbrush so that you're left with the rectangular brush head.

2 Glue the screw to the the shaft (or spindle) of the electric motor. It should be placed at a right angle to the shaft. (The idea here is that as the motor turns, the screw turns with it, producing a wobble.)

3 Glue the motor to the top of the brush head at one end, with the wires facing inward.

4 Glue the battery at the other end so that the terminals are facing the motor. The exact placement will depend on the size of the brush—the motor and battery need to be close enough that the wires can connect.

5 Connect the red wire to the positive terminal on the battery. (Ask an adult to strip the end first, if necessary.)

6 Ask an adult to cut the black wire in half and strip the end.

7 Connect the black wire coming out of the motor to the connector on the switch labeled either "input" or "load."

8 Attach one end of the extra black wire to the negative battery terminal. Attach the other to the remaining connector on the switch.

9 Flip the switch to test the connections. If the motor doesn't turn, try reversing the way you've connected the motor and the battery to the switch.

10 Glue the switch into position between the battery and the motor (it should be easily accessible from the side).

What's the Science?

The bristles of the brush act like hundreds of miniature legs. By adding the weight of the screw to the top of the motor, you produce a "wobble" every time the motor turns around. This is enough to aggravate the bristles and make them move. The movement is powerful enough to make the robot bounce off walls and other objects! The electrical circuit is called a "series circuit." When the switch is off, the circuit is broken—but when you flip the switch it completes the circuit and the battery turns the motor.

11 Set your robot free on a hard floor and watch it go!

THE SCREAMING BALLOON

Here's how to make a weird, eerie wailing sound come out of a balloon. Perfect for scaring your friends!

You Will Need
- balloon
- hexagonal metal nut

1 Take the nut and push it into the deflated balloon.

2 Blow up the balloon.

3 Tie off the end.

What's the Science?

Our old friend centripetal force keeps the nut spinning around inside the balloon for as long as we keep swirling the balloon around and around. The many sides of the nut vibrate against the wall of the balloon over and over, generating powerful vibrations that create the sound waves that make the noise. As soon as you stop swirling the balloon around, gravity will take over and the nut will fall to the bottom of the balloon.

4 Holding the inflated balloon at one end, swirl it around to start the nut spinning inside.

5 After a moment you'll hear an eerie screaming sound.

WALKING ON EGGSHELLS

Eggshells are easy to break, right? Maybe so, but they're also tougher than they look.

1 Find a space outside with a flat, level surface.

You Will Need

- 6 cartons of 12 eggs each
- outside space (this one might get messy!)
- a friend to help you get started

2 Lay the egg boxes out, end to end in two rows, with a 6-inch gap down the middle.

3 Open the boxes so you can see the eggs.

4 Check the eggs for any damage and make sure they're all pointing the same way up.

5 Get a friend to help you up onto the first box of eggs—this way you can lay your foot down flat over 6 to 8 eggs at once.

6 Bring up the other foot and walk—carefully!—across the eggs.

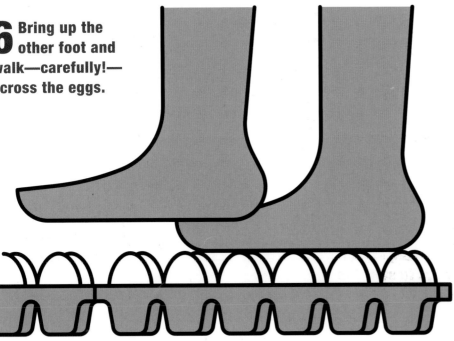

What's the Science?

The shape of an egg is a bit like the shape of an arch. The arch is one of the strongest shapes known to architecture—that's why you'll see it used in churches and cathedrals all over the world. The egg is strongest at its top and bottom, which is why it doesn't break when you stand on it. In addition, the shape of the egg helps to spread the pressure from your weight more evenly.

GLOSSARY

Not sure of the meaning of a particular scientific word or phrase? Well, you've come to the right place—let's remind ourselves what all these words actually mean!

absorb soak up or take in

acid compound that tastes sour and reacts strongly with metals

alkali kind of chemical base that dissolves in water and can neutralize acids

cell most basic building block of life. Cells are the smallest living "unit" that can survive on their own.

centripetal force type of force that acts on an object being swung in a circle. It pulls or pushes it toward the center and prevents it from flying off in a straight line

charge property of matter that can be either positive or negative

circuit path followed by electricity in an electronic device. Circuits are usually made up of wires.

condense to turn from a gas into a liquid by cooling down

conductor substance that can easily transmit electricity or heat

crystallization process of forming crystals. Crystallization is one way of separating a solid that has been dissolved in a liquid.

diamagnetic repelled by both poles of a magnet

distilled turned into a gas and then condensed to remove any minerals and other impurities. Water is often distilled.

electron type of particle that has a negative electrical charge

equilibrium state of perfect balance

evaporate to change or cause to change from a liquid into a gas by heating

frequency number of sound vibrations that occur in a second

friction resistance that occurs when one body moves against another

gravity force that attracts a body toward any other object having mass

LED (short for "light emitting diode") type of semiconductor that gives off light when electricity passes through it

molecule group of atoms bonded together. A molecule is the smallest possible version of a particular compound.

neodymium magnet type of magnet up to 100 times stronger than a "normal" magnet

neutral neither acid nor alkali

nucleation process by which bubbles or crystals begin to form in a solution

oxidation chemical reaction that occurs when a substance reacts with oxygen. For example, iron reacts with oxygen to form rust.

photosynthesis process by which plants use energy from sunlight to make food from water and carbon dioxide

phototropism tendency of a plant to grow toward the light

pneumatic machine device that uses gas under pressure to produce mechanical movement

polymer material made from long string-like molecules that has unusual properties and can be rubbery, sticky, or hard

pressure force acting over an area

reaction chemical process in which two or more substances interact with each other and are changed as a result of their interaction

refract to cause light to bend when it passes from one substance to another (for example, between water and glass)

refractive index way of measuring how much light bends as it passes from one medium to another

soluble able to be dissolved in a liquid such as water

solution liquid mixture of dissolved substances

static electricity electric charge that forms on an electrical insulator and can form sparks

supersaturated solution that has more substance dissolved than the liquid can hold. The substance will crystallize quickly if it has a scratch or speck to start it off.

surface tension phenomenon in which a "skin" forms on the surface of a liquid because of water molecules being attracted to each other

transpiration process in which plants "suck" water up from their roots and then release it through their leaves as water vapor

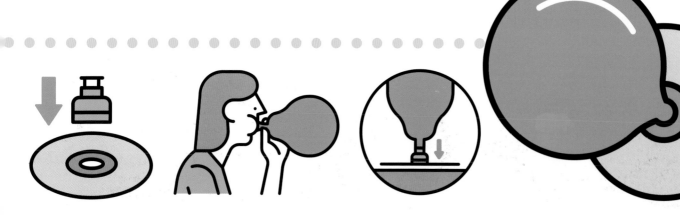

INDEX